GET
STARTED
CREATIVE WAYS TO
MOTIVATE
YOURSELF

GET STARTED

Summersdale Publishers Ltd
46 West Street
Chichester
West Sussex
PO19 1RP
UK

www.summersdale.com

Printed and bound in Croatia

ISBN: 978-1-84953-973-9

Substantial discounts on bulk quantities of Summersdale books are available to corporations, professional associations and other organisations. For details contact general enquiries: telephone: +44 (0) 1243 771107, fax: +44 (0) 1243 786300 or email: enquiries@summersdale.com.

GET
STARTED

CREATIVE WAYS TO

MOTIVATE
YOURSELF

EMMA HILL

summersdale

CONTENTS

INTRODUCTION

THE FIRST STEP IS YOU HAVE TO SAY THAT YOU CAN.

Will Smith

WHAT IS MOTIVATION?

Motivation is the desire or willingness to do something. It's the force that drives us to get things done; it's the desire to set goals and the energy and enthusiasm to pursue them. It's the difference between putting our heads under the pillow and hitting the snooze button and bounding out of bed for an early-morning run; or lazing on the sofa overdosing on TV programmes and getting out and about with friends and family. Motivation is a crucial element in defining our aims and purpose in life. And it's vital if we're going to succeed.

HOW DOES MOTIVATION HELP US?

If we have no motivation, we have no drive to complete a task or improve our lives. Motivation energises us and gives us a reason to pursue our goals and to commit to them. It we are truly motivated we will feel more fulfilled as we are able to tick off our to-do lists, realise our ambitions and embrace the inevitable challenges that come our way. If we are driven to accomplish our goals, our self-confidence soars and subsequently we feel happier and more content with life.

PRESSURE TO SUCCEED

MANY OF US IN TODAY'S SOCIETY FEEL UNDER PRESSURE TO ACHIEVE. WE MUST BE INTERESTING, SUCCESSFUL, HEALTHY AND HAPPY. WE SHOULD BE WORKING HARD, PLAYING HARDER, EXERCISING DAILY AND EATING FIVE PORTIONS OF FRUIT AND VEG A DAY. THE LIST OF PRESSURES UPON US IS ENDLESS AND CAN STOP YOU IN YOUR TRACKS BEFORE YOU'VE EVEN GOT STARTED. THIS BOOK WILL HELP YOU GET PAST ATTEMPTING TO FULFIL THE APPEARANCE OF SUCCESS AND MOTIVATE YOU TO PURSUE YOUR DREAMS AND ACHIEVE GOALS - THE ONES THAT WILL REALLY MAKE YOU HAPPY. MOTIVATION ISN'T ABOUT 'HAVING IT ALL'. IT'S ABOUT KNOWING WHAT TRULY MATTERS TO YOU AND ENSURING THAT YOU HAVE THE ENERGY AND DEDICATION TO MAKE THOSE IMPORTANT THINGS WORK. SUCCESS REALLY IS PERSONAL, SO LET GO OF YOUR EXPECTATIONS FOR YOURSELF AND FIND YOUR TRUE PRIORITIES.

LIFE IN THE FAST LANE

Motivation in the modern world, where distractions are everywhere, feels harder than ever to achieve. We have screens of every size vying for our attention, making it hard to stick to any given task. In so many ways, our lives are fuller and faster; there's no such thing as monotasking anymore and a much decreased ability to focus. We dash from one task or project to the next, preferably via the gym, in a constant flurry of busyness, phones pinging for our attention and inboxes overflowing. This book will help you sort the wheat from the chaff in your daily duties.

SO MANY OF US HAVE A TENDENCY TO SPREAD OURSELVES TOO THIN. WE TRY TO BE ALL THINGS TO ALL PEOPLE, YET A FRENZIED APPROACH MEANS WE END UP BEING NONE OF THOSE THINGS, AND THAT REALISATION DOES NOTHING FOR OUR MOTIVATION.

IT DOES NOT MATTER HOW SLOWLY YOU GO AS LONG AS YOU DO NOT STOP.

Confucius

SO HOW CAN WE FIND MOTIVATION IN THE CHAOS?

Whilst it feels counterintuitive to do so, slowing down will actually boost your productivity levels enormously. A recent study published in *Psychological Science* suggests that simply making the choice to sit back and do nothing at some point during your daily grind actually increases your commitment to a certain goal, and may even increase your likelihood of achieving that goal. So before rushing off to get everything done, first of all: breathe!

OVERCOME YOUR FEAR OF FAILURE

A fear of failure is incredibly demotivating and it can stop us from trying before we've even begun. Instead of letting it affect you, learn to accept failure for what it is: an inevitable challenge that we all have to face every now and again. Look for the valuable lessons you can learn from each of your failures, and accept them as a part of life. Failure can be a really useful part of self-discovery; learning what we're not good at is just as important as recognising what our strengths are, and it can motivate us to follow our true passions.

TWENTY-ONE DAYS TO CHANGE A HABIT?

This 21-day phenomenon derives from Maxwell Maltz's bestselling book, *Psycho-Cybernetics*, which sold over 3 million copies in the 1960s. A plastic surgeon in the 1950s, Maltz began to notice a pattern among his patients. He found that after performing surgery, such as a nose job, it would take the patient 21 days to get used to looking at their new face in the mirror. Similarly, it would take amputees 21 days to stop sensing a phantom limb. There's some debate about this, so don't be disheartened if it takes you longer than 21 days to become motivated.

A 2009 STUDY FROM UNIVERSITY COLLEGE LONDON EXAMINED THE BEHAVIOURS OF 96 PEOPLE OVER THE SPACE OF 12 WEEKS, AND FOUND THAT THE AVERAGE TIME IT TAKES FOR A NEW HABIT TO STICK IS 66 DAYS. TO FEEL MORE MOTIVATED AND ENERGISED EACH DAY MEANS CHANGING YOUR WAY OF LIVING, WHICH WILL TAKE TIME AND PERSISTENCE. EMBRACING LONGER TIMELINES, AS WELL AS BEING MORE REALISTIC, WILL HELP YOU FEEL MORE POSITIVE IF YOU DON'T IMMEDIATELY ACHIEVE YOUR AIM.

REALISING YOURSELF

Sometimes the barriers that hinder us from feeling motivated are more than a fear of failure or the distractions of the modern world. Sometimes they are far more to do with our inherent physiology. For example, it's very difficult for those with attention deficit hyperactivity disorder (ADHD), adults and children alike, to get motivated. Clinical instructor Roberto Olivardia of Harvard Medical School describes how this is nothing to do with laziness or not trying hard enough, rather that 'the ADHD brain is wired toward low motivation for everyday tasks'. It has lower levels of dopamine, a neurotransmitter involved in motivation.

ANXIETY AND DEPRESSION ARE ALSO LINKED TO LOW LEVELS OF MOTIVATION. IF YOU FEEL THAT YOUR MOTIVATION IS INHIBITED BY ANY FORM OF MENTAL ILLNESS, IT'S ALWAYS BEST TO SEEK PROFESSIONAL MEDICAL ADVICE.

"

KEEP YOUR EYES ON
THE STARS, AND YOUR
FEET ON THE GROUND.

Theodore Roosevelt

In order to succeed,
we must first believe
that we can.

Nikos Kazantzakis

WHERE DO YOUR MOTIVATIONAL ISSUES REALLY COME FROM?

If you're finding it difficult to get motivated at work, is it the job itself, the particular project you're working on or something else entirely that's the issue? If, for example, your home life isn't happy, then this is going to have a knock-on effect on how motivated you feel in other areas of your life.

DO YOU SUFFER FROM LOW SELF-ESTEEM?

Another barrier to motivation is low self-esteem. If you don't believe that you are good enough or talented enough to achieve something, it's unlikely that you'll even try. Some of the motivational exercises in this book involve you looking back and assessing past performances, focusing on positive attainments rather than occasions where you didn't hit your target or accomplish a particular goal. These will help you identify whether you suffer from low self-esteem and furnish you with strategies to bolster it.

SET CLEAR GOALS

It's amazing how often the mind flits over our achievements to focus on the negative. It is possible to train your brain to do this less, and some of the tips within this book will help you to do just that. If, however, you find that your self-esteem issues are seriously debilitating, you should seek professional medical advice to get to the heart of the matter.

Another boundary to motivation is a lack of clarity. What is it that you actually want to achieve? Identifying this is the first step along the road to getting motivated. There is no point in clutching at indeterminate straws, and no gain to be had from vague cries of 'I want to go out there and get stuff done!'. Where is 'there'? And what 'stuff'? Make your goals clear, attainable and measurable.

So where does this book come in? It will help you to form good motivational habits that will provide you with the perfect framework to just go for it!

WHY GET STARTED?

WHATEVER YOUR REASON FOR SEEKING A MOTIVATIONAL PUSH, THIS BOOK WILL HELP PROVIDE IT. WITH TIPS, INSPIRATIONAL QUOTES, AND IDEAS ON APPLYING MODERN MOTIVATIONAL PRACTICES TO THE WORKPLACE, YOUR HOME LIFE AND YOUR HEALTH, *GET STARTED* WILL BE YOUR INDISPENSABLE MANUAL FOR HELPING YOU ACCOMPLISH YOUR GOALS. DIP IN AND OUT OF THIS BOOK AND TRY TO CHANGE ONE HABIT AT A TIME – YOU'LL FEEL ENERGISED, REFRESHED AND READY TO TAKE ON THE WORLD IN NO TIME! SO LET'S GET STARTED!

The way to get started
is to quit talking
and begin doing.

Walt Disney

CHAPTER ONE

INTRINSIC
AND EXTRINSIC
MOTIVATION

If you can't fly, then run;
if you can't run, then walk;
if you can't walk, then crawl;
but whatever you do, you have
to keep moving forward.

Martin Luther King Jr

INTRINSIC vs EXTRINSIC MOTIVATION

Researchers have recognised that there are two types of motivation: internal – or intrinsic – motivation, which drives people to achieve a goal for its own sake, and external – or extrinsic – motivation which comes in the form of external reward, such as a good grade on an exam. Increasingly, research is pointing towards intrinsic motivation as the most effective when it comes to achieving long-term goals. This book will help you identify what type of motivation you should be looking for and how to get it.

THE CARROT AND THE STICK

The carrot-and-stick system is a common example of extrinsic motivation and is deeply ingrained into most workplaces, and indeed many other areas of life, including education, sport, family and relationships. If we want people to perform or behave well, we dangle a reward in front of them (there's your carrot) as an incentive, in the hope that good behaviour will be achieved and that it gets repeated. In a similar vein, we implement a system of punishment (that's the stick) in its various forms, in the hope that bad behaviour or performances will be avoided and not get repeated. This approach to motivation is used from childhood. For example, at school, gold stars are awarded for good work and bad behaviour results in having to go to the naughty corner.

CAN EXTERNAL MOTIVATION HELP?

Although often associated with extrinsic motivation, there are various methods of self-motivation that follow this traditional carrot-and-stick approach. A few of them we'll explore in this chapter and they can be incredibly effective, especially when the reward or reproach is coming from within, rather than from a boss or other figure of authority.

Several studies and modern-day motivators believe that extrinsic motivation is outmoded: for more fully rounded, longer-lasting motivation we need to also look at intrinsic motivation techniques. However, for the deeply unmotivated, extrinsic motivation can make those first steps to achievement that little bit easier.

WHAT'S THE TONE OF YOUR INTERNAL VOICE? ARE YOU YOUR OWN PERSONAL CHEERLEADER BUSTING ALL THE BEST MOVES AT THE FRONT OF THE PACK, OR DO YOU BEAT YOURSELF UP OVER EVERY LITTLE THING? IGNORE THE CRITICAL VOICE THAT CREEPS IN LIKE AN UNINVITED GUEST. BE A COACH NOT A CRITIC.

WHAT MATTERS TO YOU?

So if the secret to long-term success lies in that unseen intrinsic drive to do something because it's meaningful, now's the time to really pin down what's meaningful to you, to identify your true passions. Ask yourself the following questions: What makes me smile? What do I talk about most often? What would I do for free? What do I find effortless? What would I regret not having tried? Spending as much time as possible doing things you are passionate about will help you to become a more motivated, self-confident person.

REWARD YOURSELF

What if you're the one providing your own motivation? Don't look to others to provide that congratulatory pat on the back. Take matters into your own hands and reward yourself for your efforts. Tell yourself that once you have finished a set task you can have that cup of tea or slice of cake, take 10 minutes out to read a book or go for a walk. The huge advantage of this method is that you are incentivising yourself and looking inwards not outwards; you are relying on nobody but yourself to provide that motivational push.

DON'T ASK WHAT THE WORLD NEEDS. ASK WHAT MAKES YOU COME ALIVE AND DO IT, BECAUSE WHAT THE WORLD NEEDS IS PEOPLE WHO HAVE COME ALIVE.

Howard Thurman

FOCUS ON POSITIVITY

All too often we skip over our achievements and focus only on what we haven't managed to get through in any given day but, no matter how small these achievements may be, take note of them. Dedicate a special notebook for the purpose – it can be a glorified to-do list, a have-done list, if you like. It's incredibly motivating to look back on everything you've accomplished, and I'm not just talking about the big stuff such as landing a new job or winning an award. Remembering to take the car for its MOT, the cat to the vet and for not screaming at your sister for spilling red wine down your favourite top can all feel like big achievements in an over-stretched life.

TO BECOME INTRINSICALLY MOTIVATED, IT'S IMPORTANT THAT YOU FEEL GOOD ABOUT YOURSELF. YOU REALLY NEED TO START FROM A POSITION OF SELF-ASSURANCE, SELF-CONFIDENCE AND POSITIVITY FOR THE GREATEST CHANCE OF SUCCESS. ONE WAY TO BUILD UP YOUR CONFIDENCE IS TO RECORD YOUR SUCCESSES.

CARROT OR STICK?

What's your motivational drive: a reward or punishment? What makes you feel more motivated: the fear of failure or the promise of success? Close your eyes and imagine a scenario where you've missed an important deadline. Absorb how that makes you feel. Now imagine that you've hit the deadline, accomplished your goal and you're celebrating. Which of these outcomes is the most vivid in your mind? Which motivates you to succeed the most? Do you fear failure more than you crave success, or vice versa? Acknowledging what your drive is will help you to understand where your motivational triggers lie.

DEVELOP SELF-AWARENESS

Really focus on how different environments and outcomes affect you. Be mindful of what words and actions inspire you, what looks great, sounds great, tastes great, feels great. Pay attention to the people who inspire you and the tasks that drive you, and, conversely, the people who drain you and the events that really drag you down. The more you learn about your personal patterns – what gets you going or trips you up – the more you'll have to draw on when it comes to firing up your motivation.

DO NOT COMPARE YOURSELF TO OTHERS

There is nothing more demotivating than comparing yourself to someone else, so do not fall into this trap. More often than not it will lead to you undermining your own strengths and achievements. There will always be someone smarter than you, funnier than you, more successful than you, better travelled, more widely read… Focus on YOU. Compare your achievements only to your own past successes or failures. This can be a really useful exercise in seeing how far you've come and will teach you to look inwards for motivation, rather than detrimentally focusing on external factors.

IF YOU CAN TURN A DREADED TASK INTO A GAME, THIS COULD HELP TO TRANSFORM THE WAY YOU THINK ABOUT THAT TASK. IS IT POSSIBLE TO REDEFINE A CHALLENGE, TASK OR CHORE BY FINDING THE FUN IN IT? GIVE IT A GO! FOR EXAMPLE, USE THE TIME SPENT IRONING TO LISTEN TO YOUR FAVOURITE PODCAST OR WATCH A FILM.

CREATE A LIST OF BENEFITS

Make a list of all the rewards that accomplishing a certain goal or task will bring. For example, getting into shape will mean you can fit into that dress you've been hanging on to since 2001, or enable you to play football with the kids without hyperventilating from overexertion, not to mention all the other benefits you will gain from exercising and healthy eating. Pull out the list for review whenever you feel lacking in motivation. This is a great way of reconnecting with your motives. It's not so much about seeking extrinsic rewards to incentivise you, but more about recognising the personal rewards you'll reap.

CREATE INTEREST

Somewhere around the age of five it starts to sink in that we all have to do things that we don't want to do. For some of us, this little fact of life takes longer to assimilate, but wherever you are on the scale of acceptance with this one, don't have a hissy fit when faced with tasks that you really don't want to do. Instead, create interest. An active imagination can play a really important role in making the most mundane of tasks appealing. Tap into your creativeness and spot the interesting characteristics of a task. It's about recognising the personal rewards you'll reap.

IN ORDER TO CARRY A POSITIVE
ACTION, WE MUST DEVELOP
HERE A POSITIVE VISION.

Dalai Lama

MAKE A COMMITMENT CONTRACT

A 'commitment contract' is where you commit to a behavioural change and then establish a contract, perhaps with a partner or a friend, whereby some consequence (usually a financial one) will result if you fail to achieve your goal. The idea is that the desire to avoid the consequence helps to keep you more motivated. You could also try using a website, such as stickk.com, which allows you to effectively make a contract with yourself.

FIND A WAY TO DO MORE OF THE WORK THAT YOU'D DO FOR FREE. IS THERE SOMEWHERE LOCAL YOU CAN VOLUNTEER YOUR SERVICES? IF YOU'RE UNEMPLOYED, ARE THERE COMPANIES IN THE FIELD YOU'RE INTERESTED IN THAT TAKE ON INTERNS? OR, MORE OFTEN THAN NOT, THERE ARE WAYS TO WEAVE WHAT YOU'RE PASSIONATE ABOUT INTO YOUR CURRENT JOB. TAKE A PROACTIVE APPROACH AND MAKE THE EFFORT TO DO THIS AT ANY GIVEN OPPORTUNITY.

Whether you
think you can or
you think you can't –
you're right.

Henry Ford

PLEASURE SEEK

Find pleasure in everything you do. If you don't like your job, is there a specific project that appeals to you that you could ask to work on? Can you take a different approach or come at it from a different angle to make it more appealing? If you hate going to the gym, ditch the dumbbells for an energising dance class. If treadmills aren't your thing, go for an early-morning run around your neighbourhood and relish the peace. Find ways of making what you don't want to do intrinsically appealing and you will automatically be more motivated to do them.

IF YOU HAVE SOMETHING YOU NEED TO STAY MOTIVATED FOR THAT'S IN THE NEAR FUTURE, SUCH AS A MARATHON, IT MAY BE TEMPTING TO SHOUT ABOUT IT FROM THE ROOFTOPS. DON'T! THE POSITIVE FEEDBACK YOU'LL RECEIVE WILL TRICK YOUR BRAIN INTO THINKING YOU'VE ALREADY ACCOMPLISHED YOUR GOAL. SO RESIST THE URGE TO GET A HUNDRED FACEBOOK 'LIKES' AND STAY QUIETLY, INTRINSICALLY MOTIVATED.

The only way to do
great work is to love
what you do.

Steve Jobs

CHAPTER TWO

STARTER TIPS FOR MOTIVATION

YOU WILL NEVER
CHANGE YOUR LIFE
UNTIL YOU CHANGE
SOMETHING YOU
DO DAILY.

John C. Maxwell

CHANGING DAILY HABITS

The lifestyle choices that we make can often affect how motivated we feel. Making certain changes to your daily habits and practices can really help you to become more motivated in other areas. Decluttering your home may really help to clarify your thinking at work, school or college, and achieving success at these places can make you feel more relaxed and happy when you're at home. It's best to take a holistic approach to motivation, starting with focusing on our day-to-day routines and how they impact on our overall motivation.

GET MORE SLEEP

Sleep affects our overall health and well-being, our mood, and our ability to focus and concentrate. It's very difficult to feel motivated if you aren't getting enough shut-eye. What's enough? The National Sleep Foundation recommends we sleep for 7 to 9 hours a night. Studies have shown that even partial sleep deprivation has a significant effect on mood. University of Pennsylvania researchers found that subjects who were limited to only 4.5 hours of sleep a night for one week reported feeling more stressed, angry, sad and mentally exhausted. When the subjects resumed normal sleep patterns, they reported a dramatic improvement in mood.

EXERCISE REGULARLY

If you want to feel better, look better, have more energy, lower your stress levels and increase your motivation, it's quite simple – you need to exercise. It may be the last thing you want to do when you're drained of energy and short on time, but working exercise into your regular routine will really help you to get things done, as you'll feel more energised throughout the day. Several studies have found that exercising in the middle of the day can leave you feeling more energetic and productive for the rest of the afternoon. Plus, you'll smile more – the University of Bristol found that people's mood significantly improved on days they exercised due to increased levels of serotonin, the feel-good hormone.

AVOID NEGATIVE PEOPLE; THEY WILL DRAIN YOUR ENERGY AND BRING YOU DOWN. INSTEAD, WHERE POSSIBLE, SURROUND YOURSELF WITH POSITIVE, MOTIVATED PEOPLE AND THEIR POSITIVITY MAY WELL RUB OFF ON YOU. JUST BEING AROUND THE RIGHT PEOPLE CAN BE ENERGISING, INSPIRING AND MOTIVATING. SEVERAL STUDIES HAVE SHOWN THAT EMOTIONS ARE CONTAGIOUS, SO YOU CAN QUITE LITERALLY 'CATCH' MOTIVATION IF YOU HANG OUT WITH THE RIGHT PEOPLE.

WHICH MEDITATION?

THERE ARE SEVERAL DIFFERENT TYPES OF MEDITATION. MINDFUL MEDITATION IS WHEN WE FOCUS OUR MINDS ON ONE SPECIFIC THING OR AN OBJECT, SUCH AS OUR BREATHING, OR A PARTICULAR THOUGHT OR SENSATION IN OUR BODY. ANOTHER TYPE OF MEDITATION, MINDFULNESS OF THOUGHT, INVOLVES BECOMING AWARE OF EVERYTHING THAT IS HAPPENING AROUND US WITHOUT REACTING TO IT. OR THERE IS GUIDED MEDITATION, WHEN WE ARE TAKEN THROUGH SCENES IN OUR MIND TO HELP REACH A SPECIFIC OUTCOME, WHICH CAN BE USEFUL FOR KICKING HABITS OR BECOMING MORE CONFIDENT AND MOTIVATED. IF YOU'RE A BEGINNER TO MEDITATION, TRY AN APP SUCH AS HEADSPACE TO GET YOU STARTED OR GO TO A CLASS.

LET GO OF THE PAST,
LET GO OF THE FUTURE,
LET GO OF THE PRESENT,
AND CROSS OVER TO
THE FARTHER SHORE
OF EXISTENCE.

Buddha

GET OUTDOORS

The vast majority of us spend too much time indoors, especially those of us who work in sedentary desk-bound jobs. Well, it's time to get out there (or at least fling open the windows). If you're trying to solve a problem or come up with a brilliant idea, take a walk outside. A report by Stanford University researchers found that walking increased 81 per cent of participants' creativity, but walking outside produced 'the most novel and highest quality analogies'. Spending more time outdoors is said to improve mood and self-esteem, increase vitamin D levels and helps us to sleep better. Don't be tempted to hibernate when bursts of being outside can be really refreshing and energising.

EMBRACE YOUR INNER LAURENCE OLIVIER AND START ACTING! AND, NO, I DON'T MEAN YOU HAVE TO TAKE TO THE STAGE AND RECITE HAMLET SOLILOQUIES. IF YOU DON'T FEEL ENTHUSIASTIC AND MOTIVATED, JUST PRETEND THAT YOU DO. BY ACTING AS IF YOU ARE MOTIVATED, YOU WILL BECOME MOTIVATED. SOUNDS TOO SIMPLE? TRY IT; IT WORKS!

ADOPT A POSITIVE ATTITUDE

The benefits of being an optimist are seemingly limitless, with a growing number of studies suggesting that having a positive outlook can boost your physical and mental health, and even extend your life. A positive attitude will certainly give you the motivation and energy to accomplish goals, but what if you're naturally a glass half-empty sort of person? Can you train yourself to become an optimist? The simple answer is: yes. Make a conscious decision to look on the bright side of life and note how much more you accomplish. Your success will motivate and inspire you to adopt this positive attitude whenever and wherever possible.

CULTIVATE DISCIPLINE BY MAKING YOURSELF DO 15 MINUTES EVERY DAY OF SOMETHING THAT GOES TOWARDS ACCOMPLISHING A SPECIFIC GOAL. MAYBE IT'S EXERCISING, TIDYING THE HOUSE OR WRITING. WHATEVER IT IS, IF YOU CAN WORK JUST 15 MINUTES OF IT INTO EACH AND EVERY DAY YOU WILL IMPROVE YOUR LEVELS OF SELF-DISCIPLINE, SELF-MOTIVATION AND SHARPEN YOUR FOCUS.

" THE MORE MAN MEDITATES UPON GOOD THOUGHTS, THE BETTER WILL BE HIS WORLD AND THE WORLD AT LARGE.

Confucius

PRACTISE GRATITUDE

Adopting a grateful attitude will have a positive effect on all areas of your life. One way to bring what you're grateful for to the forefront of your mind is to keep a gratitude journal. Each night, take a few moments out for reflection and write down three things for which you are currently grateful, from the mundane (the washing machine is fixed) to the profound (your partner professed undying love). A study carried out by Robert A. Emmons, 'professor of psychology at University of California', Davis, found that those who kept a gratitude journal experienced significant psychological, physical and social benefit. A 25 per cent improvement in overall health and well-being was seen in those participants, compared to the group that focused on what had gone wrong each day.

IF WRITING IN A JOURNAL ISN'T YOUR THING, THERE ARE PLENTY OF OTHER WAYS TO PRACTISE GRATITUDE; TELL SOMEONE HOW MUCH YOU LOVE THEM, NOTICE THE BEAUTY IN NATURE, NURTURE YOUR FRIENDSHIPS OR MAKE A GRATITUDE COLLAGE WITH PICTURES OF EVERYTHING YOU ARE GRATEFUL FOR. WHICHEVER METHOD YOU CHOOSE, ADOPTING A GRATEFUL MINDSET WILL REALLY ENHANCE A POSITIVE OUTLOOK, LEAVING YOU READY TO EMBRACE EACH DAY.

Gratitude makes
sense of our past,
brings peace for today
and creates a vision
for tomorrow.

Melody Beattie

FIND TIME FOR FUN

Research carried out by Sarah D. Pressman and colleagues examined how leisure activities affect our well-being. They defined these as 'pleasurable activities that individuals engage in voluntarily when they are free from demands of work and responsibilities'. What they found was that individuals who spent more time engaging in enjoyable activities had greater psychological and physical well-being. This included greater experience of positive emotion, life satisfaction and engagement, lower depression scores, lower blood pressure and cortisol levels, and better perceived physical function. So, to work at your optimal level, no matter how busy your schedule, you must make time to enjoy the lighter side of life.

OFFER TO PET SIT A FRIEND'S ANIMAL. SEVERAL STUDIES SUPPORT THE NOTION THAT HAVING A PET CAN BE GOOD FOR BOTH PHYSICAL AND PSYCHOLOGICAL HEALTH. PETTING A DOG OR CAT FOR JUST 15 MINUTES IS SAID TO RELEASE THE FEEL-GOOD HORMONES SEROTONIN, PROLACTIN AND OXYTOCIN, AND LOWER THE STRESS HORMONE CORTISOL. IF YOU LIKE IT YOU COULD EVEN CONSIDER GETTING A PET OF YOUR OWN.

GO TECH-FREE

Or at least reduce the amount of time you spend as a slave to technology. Constant exposure to technology can overwhelm your nervous system, says psychologist Alan Keck of the Center for Positive Psychology, in Orlando. Multiscreening is not great for concentration and cognitive function. And if you spend more time staring at a screen instead of into your partner's eyes then it's time to address your priorities. As well as being potentially damaging to our 'real-life' relationships and interactions, technology can be a real distraction, with text and social media alerts all vying for our attention and drawing our focus away from the task or project at hand.

SMILE

Facial expressions don't just reflect our current mood, they influence it. So slap on a smile, even a fake one will do for starters, and feel your mood lift. That dose of happiness can help make you more productive as well. A study from the University of California found that those who were happier had a more comprehensive approach to problems; happiness improved their ability to think of more solutions than their negative-minded counterparts. The researchers concluded that this was due to the release of dopamine triggered by happiness, since the neurotransmitter is involved in learning, processing and decision-making. Is there anything easier than incorporating a smile or two into your daily routine?

CREATE A DAILY ROUTINE

Routine provides a sense of structure and familiarity, and actively and consciously building a daily routine will help to instil plenty of good habits. Once we stop and think about what we need to include in our routine we will naturally focus on the things that make us happy and are totally necessary. This way we lose a lot of the 'filler' activities that we were doing almost unknowingly. Once your routine is set and you're in the flow of it, you won't have to call on your willpower and motivation quite so much – you'll be completing more tasks automatically.

TRY YOGA. IF YOU THINK IT'S ALL ABOUT FINDING INNER PEACE AND CONTORTING YOUR BODY INTO IMPOSSIBLE POSITIONS, THINK AGAIN. THE BENEFITS ARE PLENTIFUL; RESEARCHERS FROM HARVARD FOUND THAT EIGHT WEEKS OF DAILY YOGA SIGNIFICANTLY IMPROVED SLEEP QUALITY FOR PEOPLE WITH INSOMNIA. PLUS, IT BOOSTS IMMUNITY, REDUCES STRESS AND IMPROVES OUR METABOLISM. A HEALTHY YOU IS A MOTIVATED YOU.

Motivation gets
you going and habit
gets you there.

Zig Ziglar

CHAPTER THREE

MOTIVATION AT WORK

NOTHING WILL WORK
UNLESS YOU DO.

Maya Angelou

IMPROVE YOUR MOTIVATIONAL FLOW

If you're feeling bored and lethargic at work, and like your career is headed nowhere fast, chances are you're suffering from a lack of motivation. Motivation in itself isn't something constant; it ebbs and flows naturally. But there are always ways you can kick-start it into action and many of the exercises in this chapter are going to help you do just that. Think of your goals as journeys and any motivational slumps are just bumps in the road. Instead of running your motivation down into the ground, find your own ways to put the fire back in your belly!

START SMALL

If you're lacking in motivation and don't know where to begin, simply start with a small task, such as tidying your desk or writing one page of a presentation. When you have completed that task you will feel more alert and ready to move on to the next challenge of the day. By doing this you will have created a flow – so you can ride on the wave of your motivational momentum, getting things done left, right and centre!

LIST YOUR GOALS

A very effective motivation technique is to write down everything that you want to achieve. It's amazing how putting pen to paper can bring your ambitions into sharp focus. If you're more visually orientated then create a mood board where you can pin cut-outs from magazines, photographs or images sourced from the internet that illustrate these goals. Be sure to place the list or mood board in a place where you'll see it at least once a day, and take a look at it whenever you're in need of motivation.

IT'S NOT JUST ABOUT HOW YOU SPEND YOUR WORKING HOURS THAT PROVIDES THE KEY TO MOTIVATION AT WORK. IN FACT, IF YOU CAN GO FOR A RUN, WORK OUT OR MEDITATE BEFORE YOU EVEN START YOUR DAY THEN YOU'RE GOING TO HAVE THE ENERGY AND DRIVE NECESSARY TO ACCOMPLISH OTHER TASKS.

MAKE A
HAVE-DONE LIST

At the end of your working day, do you ever look back and wonder exactly what it is that you even did? Like your wheels have been spinning but you haven't moved anywhere? Try not to lose track of what you have achieved in the blurred frenzy of a busy day. Before you pack up for the day, make a have-done list to focus on the tasks you have completed. Once you put pen to paper you'll very likely realise that you have achieved more than you thought. Bring all of those little accomplishments that you have skimmed over to the forefront of your mind and remember that every little step is an essential part of a longer journey.

GET FEEDBACK

One of the most motivating factors in any job is getting feedback. This can steer you in the right direction, help you to see that you're making a difference, hone your skills and make you feel appreciated. Who doesn't want that? If your manager isn't forthcoming with the feedback – be it praise or constructive criticism – then ask for it! Try to arrange regular meetings where you can go over recent work and request honest feedback.

ONE DOESN'T DISCOVER NEW LANDS WITHOUT CONSENTING... TO LOSE SIGHT OF THE SHORE.

André Gide

TAKE BREAKS

If the drudgery of the daily grind is getting you down, take a break from it. I don't mean pack your bags and head to the Caribbean, though good luck to you if you can manage that. Breaks in even the smallest of sizes and most subtle of forms can be incredibly refreshing for a jaded mind. So make yourself a cuppa, read a magazine and switch off your brain for 5 minutes. When you return to your desk, you will feel refreshed and ready to take on the world, or a spreadsheet or two at least.

KEEP ON MOVING. YOU MAY BE STUCK IN A JOB THAT ISN'T CHALLENGING OR REWARDING, PERHAPS THE FIRST PANGS OF EXCITEMENT ON LANDING THE ROLE HAVE WORN OFF NOW YOU'VE BEEN DOING IT FOR CIRCA 550 YEARS (OR SO IT FEELS). INSTEAD OF JUST SITTING ON IT, ENROL IN TRAINING COURSES TO FURTHER YOUR SKILL SET, LOOK FOR WAYS TO MOVE FORWARDS. YOUR COMPANY MAY EVEN SEND YOU ON TRAINING DAYS - SOMETIMES ALL YOU NEED TO DO IS ASK.

DON'T BE A PERFECTIONIST

Perfection is overrated, plus it's a real motivation killer. Focus on what's good enough for now. If we wait for the perfect moment to start something, we will never begin. If we expect perfection from others, we will never be satisfied. *Psychology Today* cites the pitfalls of perfectionism, dare I say it, perfectly: 'Perfectionism may be the ultimate self-defeating behaviour. It turns people into slaves of success – but keeps them focused on failure.'

GET TO KNOW YOUR COLLEAGUES

Your co-workers can provide a great support system on days when motivation is hard to come by. Simply being able to chat about your work-related issues can really help you to conquer them. Try boosting colleagues' confidence by praising them when they've done good work, or, if they look stressed, ask them if there's anything you can do to help. If you behave in this way towards colleagues, chances are they'll do the same for you. It's very motivating to feel as if you are all working towards a common goal together in an environment of mutual support.

STEP OUT OF YOUR COMFORT ZONE

Often the greatest barrier to achieving your potential is your comfort zone. But take yourself to that place where your anxiety levels are slightly raised and here you can achieve great things. There is, of course, a balance to be struck; push yourself too far and the anxiety will become debilitating.

Studies have shown that novelty tends to increase levels of dopamine in the brain, which is part of the brain's reward centre. Dopamine's role focuses on motivating us to go looking for rewards, and novelty increases that urge. So don't be afraid to try something new. Take a break from the familiar and watch your motivation levels soar!

STEP AWAY FROM THE CLOCK... OR AT LEAST DON'T LOOK AT IT. CLOCK-WATCHING IS SURE TO MAKE TIME APPEAR TO GO BY MORE SLOWLY. INSTEAD OF COUNTING DOWN THE TIME, WHICH WILL MAKE THE DAY DRAG, BECOME MORE GOAL-ORIENTED. WHEN YOU FEEL THE NEED TO CHECK THE TIME, CHECK YOUR TO-DO LIST INSTEAD.

CREATE AN INSPIRING WORKSPACE

What is it that makes you want to get out of bed in the morning? What gets your energy flowing? Let your workspace be a constant inspiration to you. If it's your family or loved ones who motivate you to succeed, keep framed photographs of them on your desk. If you love art, then adorn your office walls with your favourite pieces (if you work in an open-plan office, postcards from your favourite exhibition propped up on the desk may have to suffice!).

COME ON, GET HAPPY!

A study by economists at the University of Warwick found that happy workers are 12 per cent more productive than unhappy workers. So, how to generate that motivational burst of happiness? One way is to sing! Studies have repeatedly shown that singing elevates your mood and releases feel-good endorphins. Next time you're struggling to tackle a tricky task, try singing to yourself and see if it helps!

"
DON'T COUNT THE DAYS; MAKE THE DAYS COUNT.

Muhammad Ali

TAKE A POWER NAP

If you find your energy is flagging and you're struggling to stay focused on your task, have a lunchtime snooze. Whilst sleeping may seem like the last thing you should be doing when trying to motivate yourself to get things done, a power nap can really rejuvenate you. Countries such as Japan are way ahead of the game on this one after their government issued guidelines on the importance of sleep, and their health ministry recommended that all working-age people take a nap of up to 30 minutes in the early afternoon. Some offices have even installed power nap pods for workers in need of a productivity boost!

TIMING IS KEY TO YOUR SUCCESS IN ACCOMPLISHING GOALS. WE ALL HAVE TIMES OF THE DAY WHEN WE ARE MOST EFFECTIVE AND TIMES WHEN WE STRUGGLE. WORK OUT WHEN YOUR PEAK PRODUCTIVE TIMES ARE AND, INSTEAD OF FIGHTING AGAINST YOUR BODY'S NATURAL RHYTHMS, SIMPLY SCHEDULE YOUR MOST CRITICAL TASKS FOR YOUR MOST EFFECTIVE TIME OF DAY.

AVOID REPETITION

Feel like you're doing the same old work day after day? Find ways to make your work less repetitive. Divide up tasks so you're calling on a range of different skill sets in any given day. For example, don't schedule all your meetings or negotiations for one day, all your presentation writing for another, and your phone calls for another. If you can, break down your day into two- to three-hour chunks and try to do a little of everything each day. By doing this, you will stimulate different parts of your brain, which will recharge your motivation.

STRIKE A POSE

A power pose, that is. Want to feel confident and motivated? Stop slouching! Research from Harvard Business School found that simply holding a high-power pose for as little as 2 minutes increases your testosterone levels, which are associated with confidence, and decreases your cortisol levels, which are associated with stress. A high-power pose means having your body open rather than hunched up, so that you take up as much physical space as possible. Chest out, arms spread and no slouching – work that pose!

BE PROACTIVE

Unless you work for yourself or run your own company, chances are you won't be able to dictate your job title and description. However, there are always ways to tailor it to your own skills and wants. If you feel stuck in a rut, talk to your manager about how you can steer your job in the direction you'd like. People so often feel that the only way out of a job they're not enjoying is to leave. However, good communication with a manager can transform that job into something else, one in which you feel motivated and fulfilled.

TAKE A BREAK FROM ROUTINE. IF EVERY WORKING DAY FOLLOWS THE SAME PATTERN, IT'S VERY DIFFICULT TO STAY ENGAGED AND MOTIVATED. BE SPONTANEOUS AND INVITE COLLEAGUES TO JOIN YOU FOR A SLAP-UP LUNCH TO TREAT YOURSELVES FOR ALL THAT HARD WORK! BREAKING UP THE DAY TO DO SOMETHING YOU WOULDN'T NORMALLY DO IS A GREAT WAY TO RE-ENERGISE.

The more I want
to get something done,
the less I call it work.

Richard Bach

CHAPTER FOUR

MOTIVATION AT HOME

THE SECRET OF GETTING AHEAD IS GETTING STARTED.

Anonymous

HOME IS AT THE HEART OF IT

Some people find motivation in the home harder to come by than motivation at work, where the environment is more conducive to focusing on tasks and delivering measurable results. However, if we don't feel motivated at home – the place where we start each day – that lack of motivation can easily spread into all areas of life. As the base from which we launch ourselves, and the haven to which we return, our home environment plays a significant role in how we conduct ourselves when we step out into the world.

MORNING MANTRAS

Instead of hiding your head under the pillow and hitting the snooze button, why not try practising some motivational morning mantras? These will provide a positive framework for your day ahead. N.B. if you have a partner who hates mornings as much as mine does, maybe chant these internally rather than out loud to avoid frosty you-woke-me-up-chanting stares over the cornflakes. Here are a few to try:

1. 'Today, I will choose happiness'
2. 'I have all that I need to make today a great day'
3. 'My potential is unlimited'
4. 'I'm strong and capable of anything'
5. 'Life is short. Let's go!'

DECLUTTER

Researchers at the Princeton Neuroscience Institute concluded that a cluttered environment restricts our ability to focus, and limits the brain's ability to process information. So, it's time to clear the clutter from your home. This will inevitably be an easier task for some than others. If you're a bit of a hoarder, start by clearing a small space, then gradually expand your clutter-free zone one day at a time.

TAKE ALL OF YOUR UNWANTED ITEMS TO A CHARITY SHOP OR DELIVER THEM TO FRIENDS OR FAMILY WHO MAY BE ABLE TO MAKE GOOD USE OF THEM. YOU'LL FEEL GREAT ABOUT GIVING TO OTHERS AND THIS FEEL-GOOD FACTOR WILL MOTIVATE YOU TO KEEP ON CLEARING THE CLUTTER.

TIDY YOUR DESK

To create a productive working environment at home, you must first clear your desk. If paperwork piles up around you, it will inevitably distract you from the task or project in hand, as your mind wanders to its contents. Try to keep your desk an entirely clear surface, free from clutter, and store the things that you need to access regularly in easy-to-reach desk drawers. It's not only paperwork that builds up; there are only so many pens, notepads and staplers that one person needs. Clear your desk and your mind will follow!

HAVE AN EXIT STRATEGY

One that enables you to leave the house without spending half an hour looking for your keys. Set up a storage system near your front door – hooks for keys, pretty drawer knobs to hang coats and umbrellas on, a dish dedicated to loose change, a little cubbyhole for your handbag, crates to hold your shoes... Get creative and make an easily accessible home for everything that you use on a daily basis. Make leaving the house a breeze and you'll feel less stressed and ready to face the day's challenges when you get out of the door.

WHAT YOU DO
TODAY CAN
IMPROVE ALL YOUR
TOMORROWS.

Ralph Marston

KEEPING THE HOUSE TIDY

Maintaining a tidy home can sometimes seem like an insurmountable challenge. So often we are just too tired at the end of a busy day to do anything other than fling off our shoes and collapse on the sofa for a takeaway and a box set. However, just ten minutes of tidying a day will enable you to keep on top of the mess. Consider how you work best and adapt your 'ten minute tidy plan' to that. If you prefer to 'power through' then do a 10 minute tidy as soon as you come through the door from work. If you like to recharge and then start with new energy, take a timed ten minute rest and then start your tidying.

PERFORM A DAILY SWEEP – GO AROUND THE HOUSE PUTTING THINGS BACK IN THEIR RIGHTFUL PLACE. THE KEY IS TO DO THIS EACH AND EVERY DAY, AND DO IT BEFORE YOU SIT DOWN FOR THAT RELAXING GLASS OF WINE. IF YOU DO SOMETHING EVERY DAY, IT SOON BECOMES A HABIT INSTEAD OF A CHORE.

WARDROBE CULL

So many clothes but nothing to wear? Sounds like you're stuck in a wardrobe rut – time to get motivated to clear out your closet. Those skinny jeans you're keeping just in case one day you might possibly be able to squeeze into them again, that spangly number that you bought because it was such a bargain but have failed to wear even once, the dresses you haven't worn since 2001… they all have to go. Create a more streamlined wardrobe and enjoy how much more quickly you can get dressed and out of the house in the mornings.

CREATE A POSITIVE ENVIRONMENT

Your environment so often determines how motivated you feel, yet in order to create a positive environment you need the motivation to do it. It can all feel a bit chicken-and-egg. So, where to start? If you are overwhelmed by clutter, look to make small steps towards improving your environment. Light candles, string up fairy lights, put photos or paintings on the wall that make you feel happy, play music… use shortcuts to enhance your living space. Little by little you can create havens of calm in amongst the chaos and you'll soon be inspired to expand these areas.

TURN CHORES INTO A
MINDFULNESS PRACTICE

If chores seem like too much of a, er, chore, then find ways to make them more appealing. Why not transform them into mindfulness practices, so they become like little meditations in themselves. For example, when washing up, instead of rushing to get to the end of the task, pay attention to how the warm water feels on your skin, admire the way the bubbles catch the light, enjoy the simple satisfaction of making a dirty surface clean. When doing the laundry, inhale the scents of clean linen and feel the texture of different materials as you fold the clothes. In this way, chores can become relaxing, energising and a time to recharge your batteries.

CREATE PROMPT CARDS AND STICK THEM UP AROUND YOUR HOME – ON YOUR WALL, THE FRIDGE DOOR, WHEREVER YOU WILL SEE THEM MOST FREQUENTLY. IN BIG LETTERS, WRITE YOUR DAILY MANTRA: TIDY FOR 20 MINUTES – OR WHATEVER IT MAY BE. THESE CONSTANT IN-YOUR-FACE REMINDERS WILL BE PRETTY HARD TO IGNORE!

LIMIT YOUR DISTRACTIONS

Whatever you want to achieve at home – a tidy, uncluttered, calm haven, an environment where you can work, or a place to unwind and forget about work – limit the things that distract you from achieving your goal. Maybe you're just a little too hooked on social media and have to keep checking for updates and alerts, or perhaps scrolling through images of ideal homes on Pinterest is easier than trying to make yours one. Do you slump on the sofa in front of the TV before you've done your end-of-day clear-up? Maybe give yourself a screen limit in the evenings so you can spend a little time making the effort to accomplish your home goals.

GET UP EARLY

Research by Christoph Randler, a biology professor at the Heidelberg University of Education, found that early birds are more proactive than evening people, and more likely to be successful in life. Whilst not all of us are blessed with the circadian rhythm of a lark, we can all make the effort to have an early start. Even on days when you don't have to be anywhere by a certain time, get up and get moving. Don't hide from the day under your duvet, rise to embrace it. This will give you a more motivated mindset for the day ahead.

"

WITH THE NEW DAY
COMES NEW
STRENGTH AND
NEW THOUGHTS.

Eleanor Roosevelt

HOME IMPROVEMENT

Staying motivated is essential if you're going to complete all those little, and not so little, jobs around the home. Make sure you complete each job before you start on the next one. The satisfaction you'll feel on completing it will make it worthwhile and inspire you to carry on. If you find yourself in chaos, focus on the positive aspects of your house. It might be a total mess, but maybe it has amazing period features, a beautiful garden or light and airy rooms. And if it all gets too much, remember to take a break to re-energise.

TURN YOUR CHORES INTO A GAME. SEE HOW MANY MISPLACED ITEMS YOU CAN GATHER IN A BASKET AND WHOEVER COLLECTS THE MOST WINS. USE THIS AS A WAY TO INVOLVE ALL MEMBERS OF YOUR HOUSEHOLD, INCLUDING CHILDREN. AWARD PRIZES TO THE WINNER TO INCENTIVISE THEM TO HELP OUT AGAIN - PLUS A BONUS ROUND FOR PUTTING THEM BACK! THIS IS ALSO A GREAT WAY TO EASE ANY TENSIONS OVER CHORES BETWEEN HOUSEMATES.

PLAY MUSIC WHILST YOU CLEAN

Playing music can really help to motivate you to get cleaning. Create a playlist of your favourite upbeat tracks and make cleaning a welcome task, not a chore, as you sing and dance your way around the house! And an added bonus is that you're getting exercise at the same time. If you listen to music each time you clean, you'll soon clear your mind of the negative associations with cleaning, and keeping on top of the housework will start to feel like less of an insurmountable struggle.

CREATE A CLEANING SCHEDULE

Once you have a written schedule set in stone (or on screen) it's a whole lot harder to ignore. Start by making a list of all the jobs that need doing, then categorise them and work out how best to fit them into your week. Some apps, such as Unfilth Your Habitat, will do all the hard work for you – they can even import schedules into your diary!

A comfort zone is a beautiful place, but nothing ever grows there.

Anonymous

CHAPTER FIVE

MOTIVATION AND YOUR HEALTH

TAKE CARE OF
YOUR BODY.
IT'S THE ONLY
PLACE YOU
HAVE TO LIVE.

Jim Rohn

FIRST THINGS FIRST

INSTEAD OF TAKING AN ALL-OR-NOTHING APPROACH TO DIET AND EXERCISE, WHICH SO OFTEN RESULTS IN BURN-OUT, AS IT'S JUST TOO DIFFICULT TO SUSTAIN, DIP INTO THE TIPS CONTAINED IN THIS CHAPTER AND CHANGE ONE SMALL HABIT AT A TIME. TRY CUTTING YOUR ELEVENSES SNACK OR CHANGING IT TO FRUIT, OR PERHAPS MOVE TO A SMALLER PLATE SIZE TO HELP ADJUST YOUR PORTIONING. YOU'LL SOON FIND THAT WITH EACH SMALL STEP YOU TAKE YOU'LL BE WELL ON YOUR WAY TO BECOMING FITTER, HEALTHIER AND HAPPIER. THIS, IN TURN, IS GOING TO LEAD YOU TO FEEL MORE MOTIVATED IN ALL OTHER AREAS OF YOUR LIFE.

A SHIP IN HARBOUR IS SAFE, BUT THAT'S NOT WHAT SHIPS ARE BUILT FOR.

John A. Shedd

MOVE IT!

Exercise doesn't always have to involve high-intensity sweaty workouts. Just changing daily habits so you are moving around more can really help your fitness levels and turn you into a more active person. So instead of trying to find the parking space nearest the door, park at the other end of the car park, or on a neighbouring street, so you have to walk. Don't take lifts or escalators, walk up the stairs instead. Go on a long walk with the kids or your partner just for the pleasure of it. Instead of reaching for the remote, move your derrière off the sofa when you want to change channels on the TV. All these small things can add up to make a big difference.

YOU DON'T HAVE TO RUN A SUB TWO-HOUR HALF-MARATHON OR DO A SET OF BICEP CURLS IN UNDER A MINUTE TO BE SUCCESSFUL IN IMPROVING YOUR FITNESS LEVELS. DO WHAT FEELS COMFORTABLE AND NATURAL, AND ALWAYS REMEMBER THAT SLOW AND STEADY WINS THE RACE! IF YOU'RE STARTING FROM ZERO, LOOK FOR APPS SUCH AS THE COUCH TO 5K THAT BUILD UP YOUR STAMINA IN SMALL, ACHIEVABLE INCREMENTS.

REMIND YOURSELF OF YOUR GOALS

Before you start any fitness or healthy-eating regime, write down your goals. What do you want to achieve? Who or what is your motivation? Perhaps you want to fit into a certain outfit for an important wedding next year, maybe you'd like to be able to play football with your mates without running out of puff and turning purple from overexertion. Or do you long for more energy to fulfil your career ambitions or pursue a particular dream? Make a list or create a mood board with photos and inspirational quotes. Refer back to it whenever you're in need of a motivational boost.

CHART YOUR PROGRESS

For example, if your goal is weight loss then weigh yourself each morning. A study in *Annals of Behavioral Medicine* shows that people who do daily weigh-ins are more successful. Write down how much you weigh or use a fitness app to record your figures and monitor your progress. Many of these apps will provide flow charts to illustrate your progress, so even if you have a day when you haven't recorded a loss, you can look at the bigger picture and not become disheartened.

" THERE IS NO ONE GIANT STEP THAT DOES IT. IT'S A LOT OF LITTLE STEPS.

Peter A. Cohen

FIND A REAL ROLE MODEL

IF YOU'RE FEMALE, CHANCES ARE YOUR FIRST FEMALE ROLE MODEL WAS BARBIE. WITH A BODY SHAPE THAT IS TOTALLY UNATTAINABLE – SCIENTISTS HAVE PROVED THAT BARBIE AS A REAL WOMAN IS ANATOMICALLY IMPOSSIBLE – THIS IS NOT A HEALTHY ROLE MODEL TO HAVE WHEN IT COMES TO BODY SHAPE (OR WARDROBE!). SIMILARLY, THE BOYS HAD SUPER-BUFF ACTION MAN AND MUSCLE-CLAD SUPERHEROES TO ASPIRE TO. SO IT'S TIME TO RETHINK WHAT THE IDEAL BODY SHAPE IS AND FIND A NEW ROLE MODEL. A REAL ONE. A STRONG ONE. A HEALTHY ONE!

DON'T FALL FOR THE FADS

We're constantly being bombarded by horror stories in the media about foods we can't touch because they will cause incurable diseases and instantaneous obesity. We're told about an ever-growing list of glorified superfoods that are the answer to all of our health issues. Oh, and they'll help you live FOREVER! Instead of trying to absorb all of the information, or misinformation, adopt a common-sense attitude to your eating habits. Opt for a balanced diet that covers all of the food groups and includes plenty of fruit and veg. Try to avoid processed foods with their endless lists of ingredients and, instead, cook as much as you can manage from scratch. A sensible diet like this is far easier to sustain long-term than anything based on the latest fads.

EXERCISE CAUTION

Take an equally cautious approach to intense exercise regimes that promise weight loss fast. The most sustainable weight loss always comes from following a slow and steady plan, so whilst you may be tempted to embark on intense exercise regimes and super-strict diets in the run up to a holiday to get beach fit, for example, keep in mind that any gain (or rather loss) will likely be short-lived.

IDENTIFY YOUR BAD EATING HABITS

What makes you overeat, or eat the wrong things? Are you an emotional eater? Do you turn to comfort food as soon as the going gets tough? When you're stressed do you use food as a distraction technique – a way of refocusing attention away from whatever it is that's making your cortisol levels fly through the roof? Or perhaps you're overstretched, tired and you automatically reach for sugary foods in order to give you that short burst of energy you're so desperately in need of. When what we eat is so tied up with our emotions, unfortunately we never seem to crave anything healthy.

ONCE YOU'VE IDENTIFIED WHAT SENDS YOU STRAIGHT TO THE FRIDGE OR BISCUIT TIN, TRY TO THINK OF OTHER, HEALTHIER, TECHNIQUES TO DEAL WITH THESE MOOD SWINGS, PREFERABLY ONES THAT DON'T INVOLVE FOOD. IF, HOWEVER, ALL PATHS LEAD BACK TO FOOD THEN JUST MAKE SURE THAT YOU LIMIT YOUR TEMPTATIONS. DON'T BUY THE HIGH-SUGAR, EMPTY-CALORIE OPTIONS; INSTEAD, STOCK UP ON HEALTHY ALTERNATIVES SUCH AS DRIED FRUIT OR FLAVOURED NUTS.

MIX IT UP

Doing the same workout or eating the same meal may be convenient, but by stepping out of your usual routine you're more likely to retain interest and motivation. If you always go for a run, for example, try a dance class or even hula-hooping. As well as keeping things interesting, it will boost the effectiveness of your regime – several studies support the fact that workouts that challenge your body in new ways over time are the most beneficial. In the same way, try not to get stuck in food ruts. Look online for healthy recipes or treat yourself to a healthy-eating cookbook to widen your culinary horizons and keep your taste buds tantalised.

SNACK WISELY

Studies have repeatedly shown that healthy snacking improves overall health, curbs cravings, fights weight gain, regulates mood, boosts brainpower and gives you the energy you need to keep going all day. So step away from the biscuits on your tea break and, instead, keep a range of healthy snacks on your desk. Foods such as fruit, vegetables and nuts are both satisfying and packed with the nutrients, fibre and protein your body needs. Plus, they guard against sugar highs and lows, so you are less likely to succumb to your sugar cravings.

You are never too old to set another goal or to dream a new dream.

Les Brown

FEEL GOOD ABOUT YOURSELF

Don't be disheartened if you're keeping up a great healthy-eating and exercise regime but you feel as though your body isn't changing as dramatically as you'd like it to. According to psychotherapist Kathy Kater, the research on body diversity tells us that 'even if we all ate the same optimal, wholesome diet and exercised to the same high degree of physical fitness, we would still be very diverse in our shapes. Some quite thin and some quite big, but most in the middle'. So you may not look like a supermodel or a buff Greek god, but who cares? If you're exercising and eating well, chances are your skin is glowing and your wobbly bits are a bit less wobbly than they once were! Each of these steps forward, however small, are incredibly motivating.

WHY NOT FIND AN EXERCISE BUDDY? IT'S SO MUCH EASIER TO GET MOTIVATED TOWARDS A FITNESS GOAL IF YOU HAVE A FRIEND OR COLLEAGUE ALONGSIDE YOU – TO CHEER YOU ON, TO GO THROUGH THE HIGHS AND PITFALLS WITH YOU, TO MOP YOUR SWEATY BROW... OK, THE LATTER IS TAKING THINGS A BIT FAR, BUT DON'T UNDERESTIMATE THE POWER OF HAVING A TEAMMATE OR TWO ON SIDE.

Be thankful for what you are now, and keep fighting for what you want to be tomorrow.

Anonymous

DON'T DEPRIVE YOURSELF

Never go hungry. Nutritionists have proven that the biggest cause of overeating is actually under-eating – we go too long without eating, and then pig out when we are ravenously hungry. The answer to this is to eat little and often. Blood sugar fluctuates every 3 hours and if you don't eat something to raise your blood sugar your metabolic rate may slow down. Frequent small meals can help increase your resting energy expenditure (so you burn more calories) and decrease your body-fat percentage. Furthermore, eating frequently helps to keep blood sugar levels steady, meaning you'll feel more energised all day long.

RIGID DIETS DON'T WORK FOR ANYBODY. ALLOW YOURSELF THE ODD TREAT AND SAVE YOURSELF FROM SUGAR-DEPRIVED INSANITY! MAYBE JUST SET ONE DAY OF THE WEEK WHERE YOU'RE ALLOWED ONE INDULGENT TREAT. IT WILL TASTE AMAZING! NO GUILT NECESSARY. THIS WILL ALSO HELP YOU TO AVOID FALLING OFF THE HEALTHY-EATING WAGON WITH UNHEALTHY BINGES.

IF NOT NOW, WHEN?

WHEN?

Hillel the Elder

CHAPTER SIX

CREATIVITY: THE NEW MOTIVATOR

DON'T LOAF AND INVITE INSPIRATION; LIGHT OUT AFTER IT WITH A CLUB.

Jack London

WHAT IS CREATIVITY?

Rather aptly, there's no concrete definition of creativity, but most experts agree that it has something to do with the ability to come up with new ideas, new links between ideas and novel solutions to problems. It now appears that there's a strong connection between being creative and our overall well-being and happiness levels. Recent discoveries in the field of positive psychology have shown that happiness fuels success, not the other way around. When we are positive, our brains become more engaged, creative, motivated, energetic, resilient and productive at work. So being creative makes us happier, and when we are happier we are more highly motivated.

GET STARTED

So is it time to lob the keyboard straight out of the window and pick up a paintbrush? Well, that's possibly a little bit over the top – we may be trying to channel creativity here, but there's no need to go all-out rock star. The tips throughout this chapter will help you to embrace your creativity (however deeply hidden it may be) and in doing so you can increase your happiness levels and boost your motivation.

GET ARTY

Participants in a Boston College study became happier when they distracted themselves through creating artwork that expressed their negative feelings. So when you are stuck in a motivational rut, why not try painting a picture, expressing what it is that is making you feel so negative, or how you are feeling? It matters very little if you produce a masterpiece or daub stick figures and indistinguishable (OK, let's call them abstract) shapes onto the paper. What matters is the process, not the result.

YOU DON'T HAVE TO BE AN ARTIST, A SINGER OR A WRITER TO BE CREATIVE. EXPERTS CLAIM THAT ABSOLUTELY ANYONE CAN BE CREATIVE, AND ACCORDING TO A STUDY COMPLETED BY HARVARD UNIVERSITY, CREATIVITY IS 85 PER CENT A LEARNED SKILL. 'IT REALLY HAS TO DO WITH OPEN-MINDEDNESS,' SAYS DR CARRIE BARRON, CO-AUTHOR OF THE CREATIVITY CURE. SHE ALSO NOTES THAT CREATIVITY APPLIES TO EVERYTHING, FROM MAKING A MEAL TO GENERATING A BUSINESS PLAN.

GET COOKING

Cooking is a practical and domestic endeavour, yes, but it can also be an incredibly creative journey. Experiment with ingredients and flavours and create your very own signature dishes. Producing something by hand also means getting information from multiple senses at once – cooking, in particular, calls on all of the senses as we feel, smell, watch and taste as we cook – which can stimulate creative thinking. This can also become a mindful experience, as we focus on the present moment and become absorbed in the act of chopping, peeling, stirring and preparing. Cooking is a time to recharge, re-energise and create.

WRITE A SENTENCE A DAY

A 2006 George Washington University study of 300 senior citizens found that creative activities, such as art and writing, slow the aging process, resulting in fewer doctor visits and better mental health. So, as well as making us happier and more motivated, getting creative could even extend our lives! If you're not a writer and feel intimidated by the idea of writing, why not try just writing one sentence a day? You could see if a story starts to take shape, but ultimately you don't need a specific goal. Just write for the sake of writing!

WHEN YOU COME
TO A ROADBLOCK,
TAKE A DETOUR.

Mary Kay Ash

DAYDREAM

Daydreaming is often perceived as a negative habit, one that lowers productivity. However, the results of several studies contradict this notion. One such study, carried out by Benjamin Baird and Jonathan Schooler and published in *Psychological Science*, tested participants by asking them to come up with alternative uses for everyday objects. They were given two minutes to come up with the uses. After two sessions, the participants had 12 minutes where they either rested or performed a demanding mental exercise. When the alternative uses tests resumed, the people who had let their minds wander during the rest period did 41 per cent better on the retests than those who had focused on another mental exercise. It suggests that mentally walking away from a task is a good way to creatively solve a problem that you're already working on.

SOAK UP SOME ART

Being creative doesn't have to involve making something; it can also include appreciating things other people (perhaps more naturally gifted than yourself) have made. It can be about hearing, seeing or reading something amazing. Go to an art gallery and immerse yourself in the work, or read a great book, perhaps a classic novel or some poetry, whatever you may find inspiring. Listen to music. Try to listen to something that you've never heard before – there's nothing like novelty to spark creativity. Ask for suggestions from friends, or explore apps such as Spotify.

USE VISUALISATION

Several studies have highlighted the strength of the mind-body connection that link thoughts and behaviours – an important connection for achieving happiness in life. So it's time to, very literally, use your imagination. Envisage yourself achieving your goal. Create a detailed mental image of the desired outcome using all of your senses. Who are you with? What emotions are you feeling? What can you smell, hear, see? Intensify your image by hearing praise, even applause. Relish this glow of success. Refer back to this mental imagery when you need a motivational boost.

TRY THE 30 CIRCLES TEST

This creative exercise was devised by researcher Bob McKim, and is featured in Tim Brown's TED talk 'Tales of Creativity and Play'. First, you take a piece of paper and draw 30 circles on it. Now, in 1 minute, adapt as many circles as you can into objects. For example, one circle could become a sun. Another could become a globe, another a flower, a face… whatever comes to mind. How many can you do in a minute? Most people have a hard time getting to 30 because we overthink it. Try it when you're struggling with a particular task or project at work or college. It may just get your brain hooked up and your thoughts flowing again, helping you out of a motivational rut.

BEING CREATIVE ISN'T SOMETHING YOU NEED TO BE BORN WITH, IT JUST NEEDS TO BE SOMETHING YOU WANT TO EXPLORE. CREATIVITY IS SOMETHING THAT COMES INSTINCTIVELY TO ALL OF US - YOU JUST HAVE TO DETERMINE WHAT YOUR CHANNEL IS. SO GO FOR IT AND TRY OUT A FEW CREATIVE MEDIUMS. YOU MIGHT FIND YOU'RE A LOT MORE CREATIVE THAN YOU THOUGHT!

"

EVERY CHILD
IS AN ARTIST.
THE PROBLEM IS
HOW TO REMAIN
AN ARTIST ONCE
HE GROWS UP.

Pablo Picasso

FIND YOUR INNER CHILD

THIS IS NOT AN INVITATION TO JUMP IN THE BALL PIT AT YOUR LOCAL SOFT PLAY CENTRE, BUT RATHER A SUGGESTION TO SHAKE OFF A FEW OF THOSE ADULT INHIBITIONS THAT IMPINGE ON YOUR CREATIVITY. CHILDREN HAVE A NATURAL CREATIVITY, ONE THAT ISN'T RESTRAINED BY A FEAR OF WHAT THEY'RE CREATING. THEY LOOK AT THE WORLD WITH ENDLESS FASCINATION, ASKING ENDLESS (OR SO IT FEELS SOMETIMES) QUESTIONS ABOUT THE WORLD AROUND THEM. TAP INTO THAT AND TRY TO DO THE SAME. ADOPT A CURIOUS ATTITUDE AND YOU'LL FIND FASCINATION IN EVEN THE MOST MUNDANE OF THINGS. BREAK THE RULES (IN A RESPONSIBLE SORT OF A WAY) AND HAVE A LITTLE FUN. EXPLORE THE WORLD WITH NEW EYES AND YOU'LL SEE YOUR PROBLEMS, AMBITIONS AND DREAMS IN A FRESH LIGHT.

PLAY WORD-ASSOCIATION GAMES

This is a great way to loosen up your mind. It works best with a few people, so it could be a good one to try with a group of colleagues at work. If you're on your own, you can play solo by putting pen to paper; simply write down your starter word and spend the next 10 minutes saying the next words that come to mind. If you're in a group, no need to write anything down, just take it in turns to say the associated word that comes to mind. You may feel silly, but let go of your inhibitions and this can lead to some really creative thought patterns.

LISTEN TO MUSIC

According to 'The Mozart Effect', listening to Mozart can increase creativity, concentration and other cognitive functions (this inspired a generation of expectant parents to play Mozart to their unborn babies!). Some suggest this is an overblown claim, though really any music that you enjoy, classical or not, is likely to have a stimulating effect on the brain. As long as music can get you in a positive mood and increase your arousal levels, you might end up reaping cognitive benefits. Choose your favourite tracks and you'll boost mood and concentration, fire up new synapses, and enhance creative thoughts.

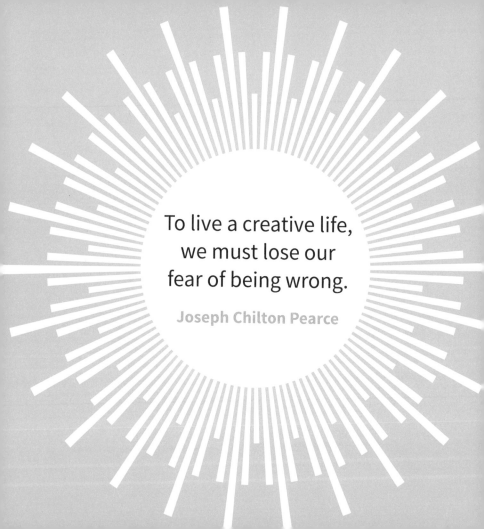

To live a creative life,
we must lose our
fear of being wrong.

Joseph Chilton Pearce

DOODLE

If you see someone doodling in a meeting, you probably think they're not concentrating, right? Wrong! Doodling can be a great way to stay focused and 'in the room'. Sunni Brown, author of *The Doodle Revolution*, notes that some of the greatest thinkers – from Henry Ford to Steve Jobs – used doodling to jump-start creativity. Doodling can enhance, recall and activate unique neurological pathways, leading to new insights and cognitive breakthroughs. So forget what they told you at school and get scrawling in your margins.

CREATIVITY FLOURISHES WHEN WE DO SOMETHING WE'VE NEVER DONE BEFORE, SO WHY NOT SIGN UP TO SOMETHING NEW? LOOK FOR EVENING CLASSES IN PHOTO-GRAPHY OR POTTERY. TAKE LIFE DRAWING CLASSES. LEARN TO DANCE, JOIN A ROCK CHOIR, TEACH YOURSELF TO PLAY THE GUITAR. OR, FAILING THAT, JUST CHANGE ONE OF YOUR DAILY ROUTINES.

Creativity involves
breaking out of
established patterns
in order to look at things
in a different way.

Edward de Bono

CHAPTER SEVEN

MAINTAINING MOTIVATION

**Sail away from
the safe harbour. Catch the
trade winds in your sails.
Explore. Dream. Discover.**

H. Jackson Brown Jr

DIRECTION

The final piece in the motivation puzzle is direction. You can have found your focus, boosted your energy levels, increased your self-confidence, adopted a positive mindset, but if you have no true direction you will falter on your motivational journey. You may now have identified and be focused on your goals, but direction is having a daily strategy in place to achieve them. Make sure that you have pinned down what you want to achieve and you are doing a little towards accomplishing these goals each and every day. Maintain your motivational flow!

MAKE MINI GOALS

Whereas five- and ten-year plans can work really well for some people, for others they are just too overwhelming. The prospect of thinking so far ahead is intimidating, plus it's tough to maintain motivation for a single goal over a long period of time, especially when having to deal with everyday distractions and other more urgent tasks. So with large or longer-term goals, try breaking them down into a series of more achievable mini goals that you can tick off along your journey. The more frequent sense of achievement that you'll feel will help to keep you motivated.

FIND A SUPPORT SYSTEM

When motivation starts to ebb, there's nothing like having a support system in place: a group of people who can help pick you up, dust you down and cheer you on. If you're a stay-at-home mum, perhaps this support needs to come from other mums who understand the pressures you're under. Equally, if your problems stem from work or study, a group of like-minded colleagues or your college peers could provide what you need. If you're trying to lose weight, consider joining a weight loss group that meets each week, or if you want to get fitter, join other people on park runs. You don't have to go it alone.

DON'T BE TOO RIGID. IF THINGS AREN'T WORKING OUT, DON'T BE AFRAID TO REIMAGINE YOUR GOAL, TO CHANGE COURSE AND ALTER THE DIRECTION YOU'RE TRAVELLING IN – THE IMPORTANT THING IS TO KEEP MOVING FORWARDS RATHER THAN GIVE UP. LET THOMAS EDISON BE YOUR INSPIRATION HERE: 'I HAVE NOT FAILED. I'VE JUST FOUND 10,000 WAYS THAT WON'T WORK.'

DON'T OVER-SCHEDULE YOUR DAY

It's better to focus on one goal that is really important to you than lots of goals that are just casual desires. If your daily to-do lists are reaching epic proportions, then it's time to rethink what it is you're trying to achieve. Look at your list and categorise it into urgent, non-urgent and fun. The only things that should be making the cut are the urgent and the fun. The rest are potentially distracting you from what your true focus of each day should be.

ADDRESS YOUR DOUBTS

Whatever your goal is, you can likely come up with a list of niggling doubts that are lingering in the back of your mind. Address the issues head-on by creating what some psychologists term a 'yes, but…' list. Simply write down all the reasons you feel will prevent you from achieving your goal. Alongside each reason, respond with a sentence that begins 'yes, but…' So, for example:

Reason 1: I'm so unfit I will never manage to run a marathon. I can barely run up the stairs.

Response: Yes, but I have over a year to train. I will start with a Couch to 5k app and take it from there.

IT IS THE SAME WITH PEOPLE AS IT IS WITH RIDING A BIKE. ONLY WHEN MOVING CAN ONE COMFORTABLY MAINTAIN ONE'S BALANCE.

Albert Einstein

FOCUS ON YOUR POSITIVE ATTRIBUTES

This is a great exercise if you're feeling defeated, and like you're just not good enough. Every morning, take 2 minutes out of your routine to write down a list of your good points. Remind yourself of why you are, or could become, superb at doing something, and why your goal is totally within your grasp. List all of your experience, skills and positive personal attributes. This will help boost your self-confidence and give you a can-do attitude for the day ahead. Use your notes on your phone to make the list – this way you can refer to it at low points throughout the day. (No talking at mirrors necessary.)

ACCEPT THAT OVERCOMING OBSTACLES WILL BE A PART OF YOUR MOTIVATIONAL JOURNEY. THE IMPORTANT THING IS TO REGARD THESE OBSTACLES AS SMALL STUMBLING BLOCKS, NOT BARRIERS BLOCKING YOUR PATH. ACKNOWLEDGE THEM, ADDRESS THEM AND THEN MOVE FORWARDS. ACCEPT THAT OBSTACLES - IN THE FORM OF EVENTS, CIRCUMSTANCES OR PEOPLE - ARE AN INEVITABLE PART OF THE PROCESS.

HAVE YOU AIMED TOO HIGH?

There's nothing to say you shouldn't reach for the stars (heck, S Club 7 insisted upon it after all), but there is such a thing as aiming too high when it comes to maintaining motivation. It's a really good idea to start off with a very achievable goal, so you can ensure early success, which will then spur you on to achieve bigger and better things. Maintain a balanced, realistic mindset by focusing your energy on short-term tasks rather than long-term fantasies. Accomplishing each of these small tasks will take you further along the road towards your dream destination in manageable, non-overwhelming, bite-sized chunks.

CREATE MENTAL SPACE

Once you've found motivation, you can't just take it for granted, you have to nurture it to maintain it. One way to do this is to ensure that you re-energise and refresh at regular intervals. It's essential to regularly take the space to restore energy and gain a sense of renewal. How you do this will depend on your lifestyle and personal preferences. Perhaps it will involve a lie-in on days off, spending quality time with family or going for drinks with friends. We all need times when we can just relax, switch off and recharge our batteries.

RAISE YOUR DOPAMINE LEVELS

There are plenty of ways to naturally raise our dopamine levels; for example, by eating the right foods and exercising. John Ratey, renowned psychiatrist and author of *Spark: The Revolutionary New Science of Exercise and the Brain*, has extensively studied the effects of physical exercise on the brain. He found that exercise raises baseline levels of dopamine by promoting the growth of new brain cell receptors. Dopamine is often referred to as the 'motivation molecule', such is its importance in boosting our drive, focus and concentration.

CREATE MOMENTUM BY WRITING DOWN TWO TASKS FOR THE DAY - ONE VERY ACHIEVABLE, PERHAPS THIS COULD BE A MENIAL TASK AROUND THE HOME, AND ONE THAT TAPS INTO A LONG-TERM AMBITION. BY COMPLETING THE 'EASY' TASK FIRST, YOU WILL CREATE A MOMENTUM THAT WILL HELP YOU TO TACKLE AND ACCOMPLISH THE SECOND, MORE CHALLENGING, TASK.

"

IF YOU CAN IMAGINE IT,
YOU CAN ACHIEVE IT.
IF YOU CAN DREAM IT,
YOU CAN BECOME IT.

William Arthur Ward

FIND INSPIRATION

Look for others who have achieved what you want to achieve. If you know them, ask for help and guidance, for any hints and advice that they can offer you. If the person is a friend of a friend, ask for an introduction so you can tap into their experience and knowledge. Search online for success stories relating to your goal or for relevant magazine articles, or try reading autobiographies of people who have achieved great things. This will make you realise that your goal is achievable. If they can do it, why can't you? Take inspiration from other people's successes.

FOCUS ON THE BENEFITS, NOT THE DIFFICULTIES

Motivational slumps often occur because we're too busy focusing on how hard any given task is instead of paying attention to how great the end result will be. Instead of focusing on the difficulties, remind yourself of why you're doing it. This will help bring your attention back to the benefits of what achieving your goal will bring. Instead of thinking about how tiring exercising is, for example, focus on how much more energy you'll have when you're fitter, and how much better you'll look and happier you'll feel.

WRITE YOUR WAY TO WILLPOWER

If you find yourself veering off-course, write a list of all the reasons why you want to accomplish your goal. Studies show that when we write by hand and connect the letters manually, we engage the brain more actively in the process. Conversely, typing is an automatic function that involves merely selecting letters, so there's less of a mental connection. The act of writing helps you to clarify your thoughts, remember things more effectively and ground yourself in your goals. So grab that quill and ink… or biro.

IF YOU'RE FEELING TRULY MOTIVATED, HELP OTHERS TO BECOME MOTIVATED TOO. SHARE YOUR IDEAS WITH FRIENDS, FAMILY AND COLLEAGUES WHO MAY BE IN NEED OF A MOTIVATIONAL BOOST. SEEING OTHERS DO WELL WILL HELP YOU TO DO THE SAME. IT REALLY IS A GREAT WAY TO MAINTAIN YOUR OWN MOTIVATION LEVELS.

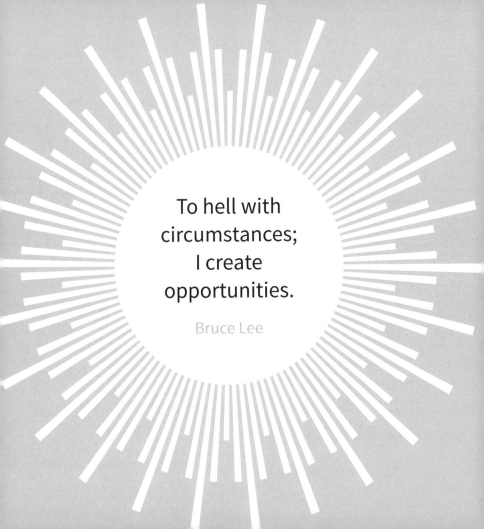

To hell with
circumstances;
I create
opportunities.

Bruce Lee

DON'T LET ANYONE TELL YOU YOU'RE NOT GOOD ENOUGH

Perhaps the biggest and most destructive hurdle you can come across on your road to accomplishing goals is someone telling you – either directly or indirectly – that you'll never make it, that you're just not good enough. Whilst sticking your fingers in your ears and shouting 'la la la' may not always be the wisest response, sometimes it just has to be done (metaphorically at least).

REMEMBER THAT, REGARDLESS OF ANY SETBACKS YOU MAY EXPERIENCE, EVERY STEP FORWARDS COUNTS. BE KIND TO YOURSELF. FORGIVE YOURSELF FOR ANY LAPSES IN MOTIVATION AND MOVE ON. ONE STEP ALONG THE ROAD IS BETTER THAN NONE. IT'S A START, AND POSSIBLY THE START OF SOMETHING WONDERFUL.

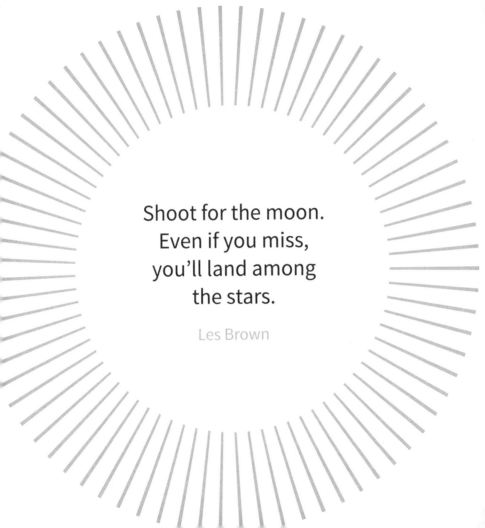

Shoot for the moon.
Even if you miss,
you'll land among
the stars.

Les Brown

STRESS LESS
How to Stop Freaking Out and Live
Life to the Full

Jasmin Kirkbride

ISBN: 978-1-84953-910-4
Hardback
£8.99

When people tell you to chill out or stop worrying, do you wish they would just shut up? Because if it was that easy, you'd do it, right?

You are not alone, and there is a way to tackle your stress Packed with tips, suggestions and quotes, this book will help give you the strength to beat the what ifs and worries and live a little more every day.

BELIEVE IN YOURSELF
Boost Your Self-Esteem and Feel Good
in the Skin You're in

Jasmin Kirkbride

ISBN: 978-1-84953-949-4
Hardback
£8.99

Do you ever wish you had more confidence in your abilities? Do you sometimes have negative thoughts, comparing yourself to others? Have you ever been afraid to speak up because you don't think your opinion is valid?

You are not alone, and there is a way to tackle your low self-esteem. Packed with tips, suggestions and quotes, this book will help give you the strength to turn negatives into positives and become more confident every day.

IF YOU'RE INTERESTED IN FINDING OUT MORE
ABOUT OUR BOOKS, FIND US ON FACEBOOK
AT SUMMERSDALE PUBLISHERS AND FOLLOW US
ON TWITTER AT @SUMMERSDALE.

WWW.SUMMERSDALE.COM